ideals®
MOTHER'S DAY

Mother's love is a precious thing
That deepens through the years,
In memory of bright sunshine days,
Of laughter, love, and tears.

Mother's love is a treasured thing;
Though far from home we roam,
The cherished bonds of faith and love
Still pull our hearts toward home.

Elisabeth Weaver Winstead

ISBN 0-8249-1051-6

Publisher, Patricia A. Pingry
Editor, Ramona Richards
Art Director, David Lenz
Production Manager, Jan Johnson
Permissions, Kathleen Gilbert
Copy Editor, Peggy Schaefer
Typography, Karen Davidson

IDEALS—Vol. 44, No. 3 May MCMLXXXVII IDEALS (ISSN 0019-137X) is published eight times a year,
February, March, May, June, August, September, November, December
by IDEALS PUBLISHING CORPORATION, Nelson Place at Elm Hill Pike, Nashville, Tenn. 37214-8000
Second class postage paid at Nashville, Tennessee, and additional mailing offices.
Copyright © MCMLXXXVII by IDEALS PUBLISHING CORPORATION.
POSTMASTER: Send address changes to Ideals, Post Office Box 148000, Nashville, Tenn. 37214-8000
All rights reserved. Title IDEALS registered U.S. Patent Office.
Published simultaneously in Canada.

SINGLE ISSUE—$3.50
ONE-YEAR SUBSCRIPTION—eight consecutive issues as published—$15.95
TWO-YEAR SUBSCRIPTION—sixteen consecutive issues as published—$27.95
Outside U.S.A., add $4.00 per subscription year for postage and handling.

d back covers from H. Armstrong Roberts

overs from Freelance Photographers Guild

I Planted My Garden Today

From morning to evening I labored
In black soil mixed with red clay;
I know the dawn will bring gladness,
For I planted my garden today.

I know I shall find some fine morning
A miracle will have come my way,
And what a glorious dawning!
For I planted my garden today.

I may never reap from my labors,
May hungry folk find food, I pray;
For I have gained solace and comfort
From the garden I planted today.

Mamie Ozburn Odum

Mother Month

May is the mother month, warming the earth.
Watch as she nurses and cuddles new birth,
Washes the morning and hangs it to dry,
Dusts with young branches the blue of the sky,
Blows on the buds till the blossoms unfold,
Warns the wee fledglings to do as they're told.
Yes, she's the mother month, and we will find
Ere she is done, she'll make all of us mind.

Margaret Rorke

Photo Oppos
GARDEN PA
H. Armstrong R

Spring's a Child

Spring is a child of golden curl,
    lips of cherry and skin of pearl.
Her breath is lilac on the hill
    where robins sing and bluebirds trill.

Her arms embrace the morning sun
    above the meadow where rivers run,
Where roses bud and bloom at will
    and a child picks a daffodil.

Spring's a child in an emerald gown
    with rainbow ribbons in her crown,
A lass so lovely I can see
    reflections of eternity.

Clay Harrison

Photo Opp
SPRING BO
Michael Ma

Mother

There is no word so sweet to me,
So full of loving sympathy
That fills my heart eternally
   As mother.

There is no one to understand
The trials we meet on every hand,
No one so noble or so grand
   As mother.

She soothes our every ache and pain;
She helps to make us well again.
She is the sunshine in the rain,
   Is mother.

She is the one to whom the trend
Of all our thoughts and love should er
She is our best and truest friend,
   Is mother.

When I am through with life's mad rac
And have reached heaven, by his grac
I want to see the smiling face
   Of mother.

Martha Cooper
Cincinnati, Ohio

Holding No Grudge

They get into an argument
About a toy or such,
But I've learned from experience
These fights don't mean too much.

In fact, although both kids might yell,
Bad feelings don't last long.
They settle it and they forget
Just who was right or wrong.

How sad it is that the adults
We children all became
Somehow **un**learned this lesson
And insist on placing blame.

And how much better off the world
Would be if we would judge
Each incident unprejudiced,
Uncolored by a grudge.

Kathleen Y. Bergeron
Mojave, California

Traded Kisses

Would you feel a bit suspicious
If a blue-eyed boy of two
Came toddling to your kitchen d
Professing love for you?

And if he slyly kissed you,
Would heaven seem so far,
Even though his big blue eyes
Were on your cookie jar?

Jo Clark O'Neil
Brighton, Massachus

Reflections

Our First Grandchild

It seems like only yesterday
I can hear my husband say,
"We have a precious little girl
That's born to us this day.

She's just as pretty as can be,
Just lying there so small."
We never realized how quickly
She would grow so tall.

Just the other day she said,
As happy as can be—
"We're going to have a little one
At the first of spring, you see!"

Now we are all preparing
As we just wait with joy
To look upon the little face
Of a precious girl or boy.

So, we thank our Heavenly Father
For his gift sent from above,
And pray for earthly wisdom
As you mold it in his love.

With love and admiration for
Your continual happy smile,
Thank you, Daughter, for giving us
Our very first grandchild.

Beverly Merritt
Hixson, Tennessee

Editor's Note: Readers are invited to submit unpublished, original poetry, short anecdotes, and humorous reflections on life for possible publication in future *Ideals* issues. Please send copies only; manuscripts will not be returned. Writers will receive $10 for each published submission. Send materials to "Readers' Relfections," Ideals Publishing Corporation, Nelson Place at Elm Hill Pike, Nashville, Tennessee 37214.

Age Struck

Who else would build a barnyard in the parlor
Or wipe the kitchen floor up with her coat?
Who else would try to mutilate a dollar
Or shove her fingers down the puppy's throat?

Who else would shovel sand with Daddy's glasses?
Or who upon a stranger's lap would perch?
Who else would eat the toothpaste like molasses
Or upset the collection plate in church?

Who else would share her apple with the barber
Or amble through a puddle for a ball?
Except the little two-year-old we harbor,
Whose name she just now scribbled on the wall!

Mary Shirley Krouse
Merchantville, New Jersey

Country Chronicle

The most treasured portraits of Mother in my album of memories are those of her tending her beds of flowers, a trowel or hoe in hand. My mother was a hard-working farm woman and mother of nine, but she loved all flowering plants and always found time to nurture them with tenderness and care.

She had the usual varieties of cultivated blooms—pansies, four-o'clocks, phlox, hollyhocks, bleeding hearts, and roses—but her greatest admiration was for the wild varieties she had brought from the woods and transplanted in plots on our lawn and in rows by the pasture fences. Along some of the stone fences were beds of pinxters, bittersweet, bloodroot, violets, woodbine, and wild clematis. She had also transplanted beds of lilies of the valley, Dutchman's breeches, hepaticas, trillium, lady's slippers, and jack-in-the-pulpit. Along the east side of the house, a bank of green stretched from one veranda to another, where ferns offered a haven for toads seeking shelter and shade. Each bed was tended with care and love.

Each year, as I watch the earth nurturing tender plants back into bloom, I am reminded of the tender love my mother had for each of her plants. By her example, she bestowed on me something very special and dear—a love for nature and for the ways of the woodlands. Mother left a legacy of love for the hills, for forest and fields. She taught me to cherish even the most common things, such as pasture stones with their lichen of delicate traceries and the songs of the birds. She taught me to love brooks and streams, whose murmuring waters sing lullabies as soothing as the ones she used to sing. She endowed me with a love of the countryside as constant and sure as the returning blooms of spring. And as the warmth of May nurtures a spreading canopy of flowers, I recall that treasured portrait of my mother and celebrate everything she taught this countryman.

Lansing Christman

John Slobodnik

Mother's Flower Bed

Underneath the arbor
Of roses crimson red
Lies a touch of magic beauty—
'Tis Mother's flower bed.

Dutchman's breeches, violets,
Buttercups of richest gold,
Dainty lily of the valley
Nestled in a hidden fold.

The royal lilac clusters
Fill the air with sweet perfume,
And the scarlet-throated poppies
Seem to dance a merry tune.

Delicate, soft pink cosmos
Look good enough to eat,
And the tiny cheerful pansies
Are bobbing at my feet.

There's nary a nook or corner
From spring till end of fall
That's not in radiant glowing bloom
As lovingly she tends them all.

Ruth H. Underhill

Photo Oppos
MOTHER'S FLO
Fred Sieb

AMERICAN CROSSROADS

Editor's Note: "American Crossroads" is a regular feature of *Ideals*, presenting photographs, stories, and jokes which have been submitted by our readers, about uniquely American events or experiences. If you have a 50 to 75 word account or photograph of an unusual or interesting occurrence unique to an American lifestyle or heritage, we would like to know. Send your submission to "American Crossroads," c/o Ideals Editorial, P.O. Box 141000, Nashville, TN 37214-1000. Please send only copies of manuscripts and duplicates of photographs or slides since submissions will not be returned. We will pay $10 for each printed submission.

Photo courtesy of the Parke County, Inc. Tourist Information Center

Indiana's rustic Parke County (centered around Rockville) has more covered bridges (thirty-four) than any other county in the nation. Each year since 1957, Parke Countians have celebrated that uniqueness with a festival beginning on the second Friday of October and continuing for ten days. Visitors can view bridges in tour buses or in their own cars by following one of five color-coded routes.

The Rockville square is a colorful festival of sights and smells where the tourist can wander through displays and demonstrations of old time crafts, a flea market, art show, and mountains of country produce while munching on homemade goodies from recipes of yesteryear. A nearby turn-of-the-century village, an antique show, a melodrama, square dancing, and other extensions of the festival in surrounding communities round out this delightful celebration.

Joyce Lakey Shanks
Terre Haute, Indiana

The Longaberger family of Dresden, Ohio, has a unique family tradition: basket weaving. When John Longaberger apprenticed his fifteen-year-old son, J.W., in the trade of weaving splint baskets (which must be made by hand from strips of wood), he had no idea he was beginning a family tradition which would continue for more than 100 years.

Father and son worked for the Dresden Basket Company, where J.W. grew to care deeply about his craft. He left high school to work full time, and when the depression caused the company to close, J.W. tried unsuccessfully to make a living weaving baskets in his home. He had to work at a paper mill during the day, but he continued to make baskets at night, determined to keep the handicraft alive.

J.W. taught his twelve children to weave also, insisting on a high quality of work for each basket. Paper bags and cardboard boxes began to take the place of baskets, however, and the children moved into other professions. J.W. refused to abandon basket weaving, and continued to make baskets for his friends and relatives as gifts. J.W.'s determination finally paid off when, in 1973, his son David noticed the number of baskets being sold by department stores. David and J.W. reopened the home business, and J.W. lived to see the quality he insisted on putting into his baskets rewarded once again. Since David's daughter is also involved, J.W.'s dream of continuing a dying craft has become a family tradition of four generations.

Jaime MacPherson
Nashville, Tennessee

Morning Vigil

In the early hours of morning
When the dew is on the grass
And the earth, expectant, silent,
Waits for dawning time to pass,
Here I walk my garden pathways
Where the fragrant flowers disclose
Secrets of inspiring beauty,
Thoughts from mignonette and rose.

Oh, the lovely things they tell me,
Silent but true and clear,
And my eager inner spirit
Is responsive as I hear
Messages of God's sure bounty,
His provision for each need
Of the soul and body hunger...
Joy flows through me as I heed.

Oh, my garden is God speaking;
From this tryst I go forth free
To the duties that are calling,
To the work he has for me.
When the tasks seem long and dreary
And my spirit is hard-pressed,
I relive the morning vigil;
And remembering, I am blest.

Della Adams Leitner

My Mother's Hands

My mother's hands were never still;
So many varied chores had she.
How comforting when I was ill,
They soothed my brow and steadied me.

Sometimes, when I am by myself,
Memories take me back to when
Her hands filled every oven shelf
With kneaded bread to bake, and then

To other chores, in our backyard
She plucked her garden's yield each day.
No task to her seemed dull or hard,
For each she did in loving way.

My mother's hands were never still;
They scoured and sewed till late each night.
I see her yet, I always will,
Queen of the home she made happy and bright.

Dorothy Bettencourt Elfstrom

My Mother's House

My mother's house has always seemed enchanted,
Perhaps because I've never known the rooms
To echo any sound but gentle music
Or be without a bowl of garden blooms;

Perhaps because the doors are always open
To welcome anyone who passes by;
Perhaps because the kitchen's never lonely
For homemade bread or apple pie;

Perhaps because the windows always glisten
And let the warm, sweet sunshine twinkle through.
Perhaps my mother's gracious way of living
These years has made her house enchanted, too.

Mary Shirley Krouse

Photo Overleaf
MOTHER'S KITCHEN
Fred Sieb

My Favorite Teapot

I have a favorite teapot and
I just cannot record
The many cheery cups of tea
This old teapot has poured.

When friendly guests come by to chat
Upon a winter's day,
A steaming pot of fragrant tea
Can chase the cold away.

It must recall the happiness
That it has given me
By faithfully brewing for my guests
Delicious cups of tea.

Carice Williams

The Copper Teakettle

It's made so many cups of tea—
They can't be counted easily—
For neighbors stopping by to sit,
To chat and laugh with Mom a bit.

Its happy whistle could be heard,
Like music to each spoken word,
As Mom would pour a fragrant cup
That seemed to perk poor spirits up,
Then lend an understanding ear
To problems she would often hear:
Domestic ones or otherwise,
That brought warm tears to worried eyes.

And now the kettle means to me
How nice good fellowship can be:
A cup of something warm to share
With someone sweet who's always there.

Vivian Marie Chatman

Mother's Day Brunch

Breakfast Croissant Sandwiches

Makes 4 servings

4 **croissants, warmed and split in half**
4 **omelets**
4 **large mushrooms, thinly sliced**
2 **avocado slices**

Layer all ingredients into croissants.

Variations

Ham and cheese: Substitute omelets and mushrooms with 8 ounces sliced ham, 4 slices Swiss cheese, and 8 ounces sliced pineapple.
Bacon, Lettuce, & Tomato: Substitute omelets and mushrooms with 8 cooked bacon strips, 4 lettuce leaves, and 4 tomato slices.

Fruited Bibb Salad

Makes 4 servings

2 **small heads Bibb** *or* **butterhead lettuce**
½ **avocado, sliced**
2 **oranges, peeled, seeded, and sliced into rounds**
Yogurt Dressing

Separate lettuce into leaves. Arrange avocado and orange slices attractively over lettuce. Top with Yogurt Dressing.
Note: Slices of peaches, papaya, nectarines, or grapefruit may be substituted for oranges.

Yogurt Dressing

Makes 1 cup

1 **cup plain yogurt**
¼ **cup orange juice**
2 **teaspoons grated orange peel**
Fructose to taste
Dash ground cloves

Stir all ingredients together. Let dressing stand at least 15 minutes to blend flavors.

Variation

Ginger Yogurt: Omit orange peel and cloves. Add ½ teaspoon minced fresh ginger.

Omelet

Makes 4 servings

4 **eggs, separated**
¼ **teaspoon salt**
¼ **teaspoon cream of tartar**
2 **tablespoons water**
1 **to 2 teaspoons butter**
½ **to 1 cup topping of your choice**

Preheat oven to 350°. Beat egg whites with salt and cream of tartar at high speed until stiff, but not dry. Beat yolks with water at high speed until thick and lemon-colored, about 5 minutes. Fold yolks into whites. Heat butter in 10-inch omelet pan over medium heat until just hot enough to sizzle a drop of water. Pour in omelet mixture and carefully smooth the surface. Cook until puffy and lightly browned on the bottom, about 5 minutes. Bake in oven for about 10 minutes, or until a knife inserted in the center comes out clean. Cover surface with chosen topping. Cut in half or in wedges to serve. Garnish as desired.

Topping Variations

Italian Sausage: Cook, drain, and crumble 2 Italian sausages. Combine with 1 large tomato, diced, and 2 tablespoons chopped fresh basil *or* 1 tablespoon dried basil. Ladle over omelet; sprinkle with grated Romano.
Light Lox: Drain and chop 2 slices smoked salmon (lox). Combine with 4 ounces Neufchatel cheese until mixed. Spread on omelet. Sprinkle omelet with lemon juice and chopped chives.
Healthy Melissa Crisp Vegetable-Garden Patch: Sauté or steam 1 cup sliced fresh vegetables of your choice. Garnish with lemon wedges.

Chilled Strawberry Soup

Makes 4 servings

5 **cups strawberries, hulled and washed**
¼ **cup sugar**
½ **cup orange juice**

Puree strawberries in food processor or blender. Pour into large container. Stir in sugar and orange juice. Chill 2 to 3 hours before serving.

Photo Opposite
ER'S DAY BRUNCH
Gerald Koser

Mother's Home

Content with little sunny rooms,
With kitchens clean and bright,
A rocking chair beside the hearth
And shelter in the night.
The shiny stove and Dad's old chair,
A mat beside the door,
Gay flowers on the windowsill,
A clean old painted floor.

She wears a starched red cotton dress,
An apron trimmed with lace,
Soft hair that makes a sort of frame
Around her quiet face.
She has a few old trusted friends,
Her love is safe and near,
A steady gracious soul that shines
From eyes serene and clear.

She makes such fragrant homemade bread,
Her pickles and her jam,
She's always cooking something nice...
A spicy home-cured ham.
Her garden is a friendly place
Of sweet old-fashioned bloom,
Where mignonette and marigold
Are heavy with perfume.

Could life hold more than little homes
Secure from greed and spoil,
The quiet beauty of the stars,
The fragrance of the soil.
A heart at peace with all the world,
Content with simple things...
She holds within her quiet rooms
The best that heaven brings.

Edna Jaques

Familiar Things

We cling to old familiar things:
Old dishes that our mothers had,
Old chairs and rugs and patchwork quilt
A jackknife that belonged to Dad.
They seem to speak in quiet tones
Of love that is for us alone.

How dear a cup or plate can grow
When loving hands have brought it ther
And still it stays when they are gone
A household treasure loved and rare.
Even the doorknobs have a touch
Of Mom, who handled them so much.

A bit of vine she planted there
Grows beside the kitchen door,
A sunny window that she loved,
A string of scarlet beads she wore;
Through life's dull monotone it sings
The love of old familiar things.

Edna Jaque

My Mother's Thimble

[A]n old silver thimble, worn thin with work,
[O]n a finger whose duty was never shirked.
[It] glinted and shone as if happily placed,
[M]aking loved ones' clothes with its
　　merry fast pace.

[It] wove a pattern of girlish dreams
[A]s it made a quilt or felled the seams
[O]f a wedding gown with handwork so fine,
[F]or the stitches formed in a steady line.

[A] thimble is sort of an intimate thing,
[A]lmost as beloved as a wedding ring.
[R]eminding me of forgotten scenes
[O]f parties, events, and long ago dreams.

Grace M. Naegeli

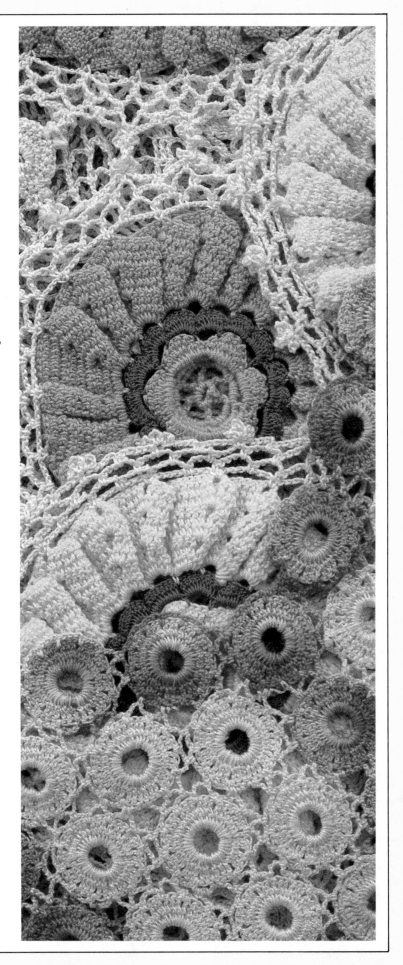

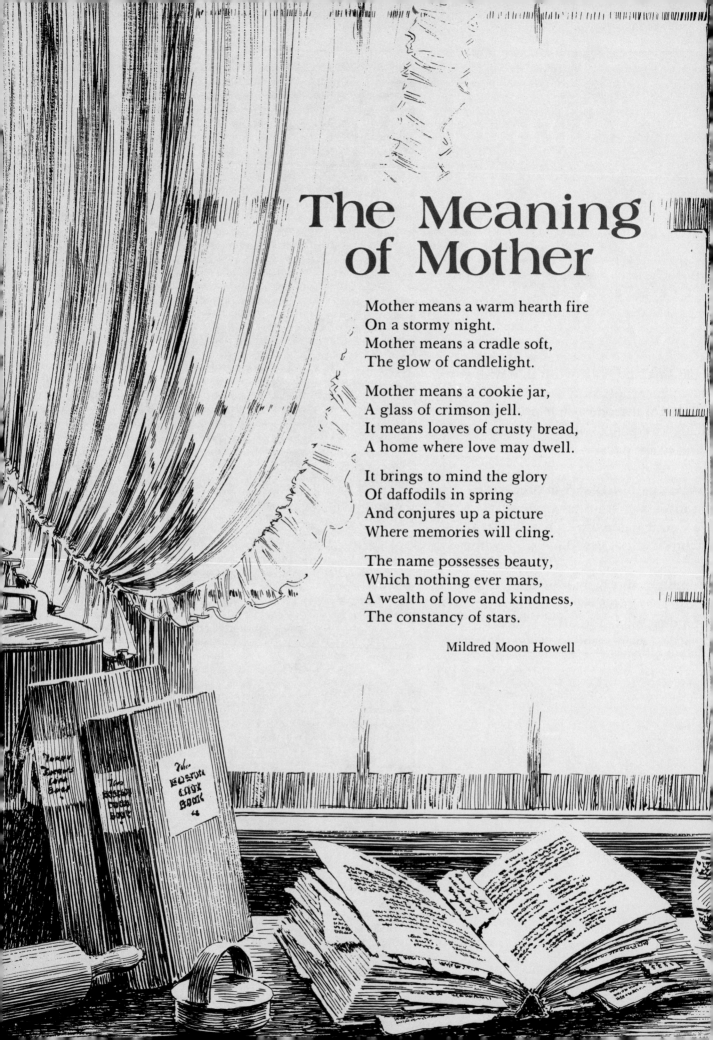

The Meaning of Mother

Mother means a warm hearth fire
On a stormy night.
Mother means a cradle soft,
The glow of candlelight.

Mother means a cookie jar,
A glass of crimson jell.
It means loaves of crusty bread,
A home where love may dwell.

It brings to mind the glory
Of daffodils in spring
And conjures up a picture
Where memories will cling.

The name possesses beauty,
Which nothing ever mars,
A wealth of love and kindness,
The constancy of stars.

Mildred Moon Howell

Mother's Kitchen

A gingerbread cookie can carry me back
To a kitchen I knew long ago,
And my mother's light footsteps still sound in my ears
As she hurried about, to-and-fro.

The kitchen was big and a little girl felt
It was just the place she should stay,
While Mother made cookies or good homemade bread
On a cold, snowy, blustery day.

In the long summer days, when the afternoon sun
Was too hot, we would play for awhile
On the bright polished floor, with jacks and a ball
As we basked in the light of her smile.

The little girl now is a woman grown,
Yet a gingerbread cookie can bring
Back the old-fashioned kitchen where Mother was queen
And her love for us blessed everything.

Kay Wissinger

The Girl That I Used to Be

She came tonight as I sat alone,
The girl that I used to be.
She gazed at me with her earnest eyes
And questioned me reproachfully.

"Have you forgotten the many plans,
The hopes that were held for you;
The great career, the splendid fame,
And the wonderful things to do?

"Where is your mansion of stately height,
With its gardens surpassing fair?
The silken robe that was planned for you
And the jewels for your hair?"

And as she talked, I was very sad
For I wanted her pleased with me,
This slender girl from the shadowy past,
The girl that I used to be.

Then gently arising I took her hand
And guided her up the stair,
Where peacefully sleeping my babies lay,
Innocent, sweet, and fair.

I told her that they were my only gems,
And precious they are to me;
That my silken robe is motherhood
Of happy simplicity.

That my mansion of stately height is love,
And the only career I know
Is serving each day within sheltering walls
The dear ones who need me so.

And as I spoke to my shadowy guest,
She smiled through her tears at me,
For I saw that the woman that I am now
Pleased the girl that I used to be.

Author Unknown

A Mother's Dreams.

They think because I stay at home
And sweep and dust the floor,
I never think of anything
Beyond my kitchen door.

They think me deaf to messages
Of winds in trees that bend,
But I think of many, many things,
While all I do is mend.

'Tis true my body dwells at home
While dear old friendships call
The loving heart and soul of me,
Beyond these humble walls.

And so I sing and bake my bread,
And sew my patchwork seams,
And while I put my bread in pans,
My heart is light with dreams.

Mary Quimby Sine

My Heart Sings

Do not pity me, I pray,
If I spend the livelong day
Washing dishes, sweeping floors,
Answering telephone and doors.

Though as busy as can be,
Deep within the heart of me
Is a joyous, lilting song,
Singing, singing, all day long...

Of the things I plan to do,
Something different, something new,
Places I shall some day go,
People I shall some day know,

Laughter in a loved one's eyes,
April showers and azure skies,
Shadows on the garden wall,
Bits of praise I can recall.

Of such things my glad heart sings,
As each hour some duty brings.
Surely now you plainly see
Why you need not pity me.

Caroline Wyatt

I Wish I'd Known My Mother When

I wish I'd known my mother
When she was just a girl.
I'm sure my father thought her
The sweetest in the world.
I know he asked her father
Before they set the date,
Then Mother wore her diamond
To show that she would wait.

Mother's trousseau had to be
A handmade work of art.
There must have been a dozen
New suits and gowns to start.
Linens, cross-stitch, appliques,
Fine quilts of blue and gold,
Most of all, her wedding gown
Was lovely to behold.

I wish I had been present
At Hillside Church that day
To hear them sing "O Promise Me,"
And brush their tears away,
To kiss the happy couple
When it was time to go.
I wish I had been present
With lots of rice to throw.

Their honeymoon was special;
They caught the westbound train.
I could have waved good-bye then
And kissed them once again.
I would have asked the porter
To give them tender care;
I'm sure he guessed their secret
(The rice was in their hair).

I know they bought a cottage
Just large enough for two.
My mother dusted it with love,
Baked sugar cookies, too.
I wish I'd been her neighbor,
Who came for snacks and teas,
Who talked across the back fence,
Exchanging recipes.

I recall when I was small
She taught me prayerfully.
Sometimes I think my mother was
A little bit like me.
Of all the people in the world,
Much more than any other,
I wish I might have known her
Before she was my mother.

Brenda Leigh

Photo Opposite
CARNATIONS FOR MO
Gerald Koser

Happy Mother's Day

We love you,
Mother!

Sixteen

She scorned such things as frilly frocks,
Hair ribbons, lace, and curls.
She much preferred the boy next door
To dolls and little girls.
To birthday parties, he would bring
Her baseball bats or guns;
All the gifts he gave to her
Were always treasured ones.

Today, another party and
Another birthday cake
With sixteen candles—sixteen years!
I prayed that for her sake
He would not tease her when he saw
Her party dress and pearls.
How could a young boy understand
What "sixteen" means to girls?

His secret code knock on the door
(The one he's used for years)
Brought sudden shyness to her eyes
And to my own, quick tears.
A tall lad entered quietly.
Somewhere along the way,
I'd failed to see the change in him;
He brought her flowers today.

Mary Lynn Nelson

Angels in Pigtails

They're angels in pigtails
but we call them girls.
Some come with freckles
and some come with curls.

They're bundles of ribbons
with bows in their hair,
And our smiles seem to linger
long after they're there.

They're fresh as a daisy
at bedtime, it seems,
As they share with the sandman
such wonderful dreams.

They're rainbows and sunshine
in satin and lace,
And the mem'ries they leave us,
the years can't erase.

They're angels in pigtails,
so precious and dear,
And I'll tell you a secret—
they're worth every tear!

Clay Harrison

Painting Opp
THE PIANO LE
John Walte

My Garden

My garden holds no vegetables,
Though I have planted seeds
In furrowed rows and tiny hills
And hoed out all the weeds.

My garden holds no vegetables,
For every time they sprout,
My little fellow takes his rake
And puts each one to rout.

Sometimes he gathers up the spoils
And brings them in a pan;
"Your bejtables are ready now,"
Proclaims my little man.

I gather him against my heart
Where, hourly, he grows;
My garden holds no vegetables,
But just a precious rose.

Helen Louise Williams

Hidden Treasures

Baseball cards and rusty nails,
A plastic boat with broken sails;
Gum and marbles, stones and string,
Rubber bands and a decoder ring;

Spinning tops and ice cream sticks,
Calendar sheets and a watch that ticks;
A rich selection to swap away
At the park playground on Saturday.

Small treasures bringing endless joy
To excite the heart of girl or boy,
Hidden snugly until Mother cleans
The pockets of those faded jeans.

Elisabeth Weaver Winstead

Her First Cake

Her twinkling eyes alight with joy;
  She scanned my old cookbook,
Announcing in a voice of pride
  That she would be the cook.

We chose a special recipe
  For little hands turned eight;
'Twas luscious golden gingerbread
  To dress the willow plate.

A gingham apron I then tied
  About her wiggling waist,
And watched as bowl and spoon were turned
  In happy childhood haste.

She did not want my help to stir
  The batter which grew tough
For tiny hands, but toiled along
  Till it was smooth enough.

The pans were greased, the batter poured,
  And then the precious cake
Was placed inside the oven hot,
  Where it could gently bake.

And when it came out high and light,
  On smiles she took a lease
And ran to show the family
  Her golden masterpiece.

And as I watched her earnest face,
  In thoughts my prayer was said,
Please help her keep the good in life
  High as her gingerbread.

Helen Barker

Photo Op
NEW C
Bob Ta

Feathering Her Own Nest

My daughter's first home of her own, a small efficiency apartment, gives me a comfortable feeling. It looks like her. Sitting here beside my small suitcase, I scan the room.

Hanging on the wall above her neatly organized desk, where I recall seeing her sit for hours writing her high school term papers, are the letters C,A,T,H,Y in a vertical string. The summer I worked those bright orange needlepoint letters for her dorm room, I must have wondered: Would she graduate from college? Would she find a job?

Now, sipping on a cup of tea from a heart-covered mug we sent her one Valentine's Day, I remember Cathy's great announcement of last year:

"I'll have a job in a big city before I graduate in May."

Her dad and I had our doubts, but we sure liked her optimism.

She did it, as advertised. Landed the job after a hundred or more interviews and enough rejection letters to cover a whole wall. And we let out a sigh of relief!

Laughing to myself, I place my cup on her kitchen table, formerly my kitchen table.

Can this be the same child I walked to kindergarten every day for six weeks until I finally convinced her she could walk the path alone? Can she now actually be out in the world selling business forms?

"I'm off to see a prospective client," says the same girl who hesitated to answer the phone at eight for fear she might not know the caller.

"Make yourself at home," she tells me as she stands, briefcase in hand, dressed in a tailored suit of light gray, a pin-striped blouse, a skinny charcoal bow at the neck.

Putting the briefcase down, she reaches out. We hug. Tightly. Then let go.

"Bye," she says, giving me a look that said what we couldn't say to one another. That we wouldn't see one another again for months.

"Say hi to Dad. To everyone," she said.

"Sure, I will," I said, grabbing another hug. "Bye, honey," I said softly as a football climbed my throat.

A last glance. A smile. Then she headed out the door, briefcase in hand. A part of me went with her.

Now, looking around the place that is her alone, the past leaps out at me. The sleeping bag she slept in last night so I could have her bed went on many trips to camp, on numerous overnights and is still filled with the giggles of Cathy's childhood.

Sitting on that flowered sleeping bag at age ten, surrounded by friends, her happy voice rang out. I listened as she started a new ghost story. Could I possibly have imagined the Cathy of today? No, probably not.

Back then, when I thought I'd never get any sleep, that the girls and their giggle fits would last forever, there was no way I could foresee the sophisticated young lady who handed me one of her business cards as we chatted at the breakfast table this morning.

Lying on her coffee table, the one her Dad and I purchased the year she was born, right beside the scratch she made with her twirling baton, are copies of *Business Week* and *Time*.

She tossed out her huge stack of *Seventeen* issues when she visited home between graduation and the start of her new job. She packed all of her belongings, plus a few of ours.

We watched Cathy pull out of the driveway, a U-haul trailer behind her. Watched as she left to begin a new life on her own.

Months later, when I arrived for my overnight visit, the towels lay on the bed just the way I always put them out for her on trips home from college.

She served me a cold drink. Hung up my dress. Offered me a snack. Made me feel at home in her home. It was like watching a movie of myself.

Our visit was short, but we covered a lifetime of memories. Shared thoughts. Ideas. Hopes and dreams for the future.

We went out to dinner and shared much more than the food before us. She drove me around her city, introduced me to some of her friends. Then we headed back to her place and shared more conversation, highlighted by brief visits to days gone by.

Climbing into bed, resting on the striped sheets of blue, the ones we purchased the day she fell off the balance beam and chipped her front tooth, I sighed. I said goodnight to my daughter, and then fell into a deep and happy sleep.

And now it's time for me to leave. Placing down a box of creamy chocolates that I purchased when I took a walk after she left, I glance around once more. I grab a pen, a piece of note paper from the desk top and write a note.

"Bye. Thanks for the fun visit. Love your apartment. We are so PROUD of you. Take care. Love, Mother.

"P.S. Water the plant I brought twice a week. Don't forget!"

I add a crooked smiley face.

And now, heading out the door, I again feel the hug she gave me earlier. I take it with me as I leave her home and head for mine.

Lisbeth J. Thom

So Little Did I Realize

I wonder where you are today,
Sweet child of only seven,
With curly locks of reddish hue
And eyes as blue as heaven.
How oft you sat upon my lap,
"I love you, child," I'd say;
  So little did I realize
  How time would slip away.

I wonder where you are today,
Sweet miss of seventeen,
With baby days and childish ways
Now vanished like a dream.
I still recall your smiling face
On graduation day;
  So little did I realize
  How time would slip away.

I wonder where you are today,
Sweet bride of twenty-one;
Perchance the Lord will bless you
With a daughter or a son.
Upon your lap oft hold that child
For soon, like Mom, you'll say,
  "So little did I realize
  How time would slip away."

Loise Pinkerton Fritz

On the Wings of Night

On the wings of the night, I passed
The house where I first wept and laughed,
And felt the wind on meadow grass
In the clarity of morning
When hills were lilac blossoms stacked
And hurts were mended by a kiss,
And hopes were bright as daisy chains,
And dreams, a singing of flamebirds,
And love, a tender sheltering
'Neath a star in the crib window.
But, ah, now I cannot tarry;
My heart's beating too busy fast
For that wonder in the dawning
Of joy new as the early dew.
Only the astonished glimpse back
As I hasten, hasten onward.
Poor wayworn pilgrim—be dazzled!
There is still time—aye, dear, still time.

Mary Roelofs Stott

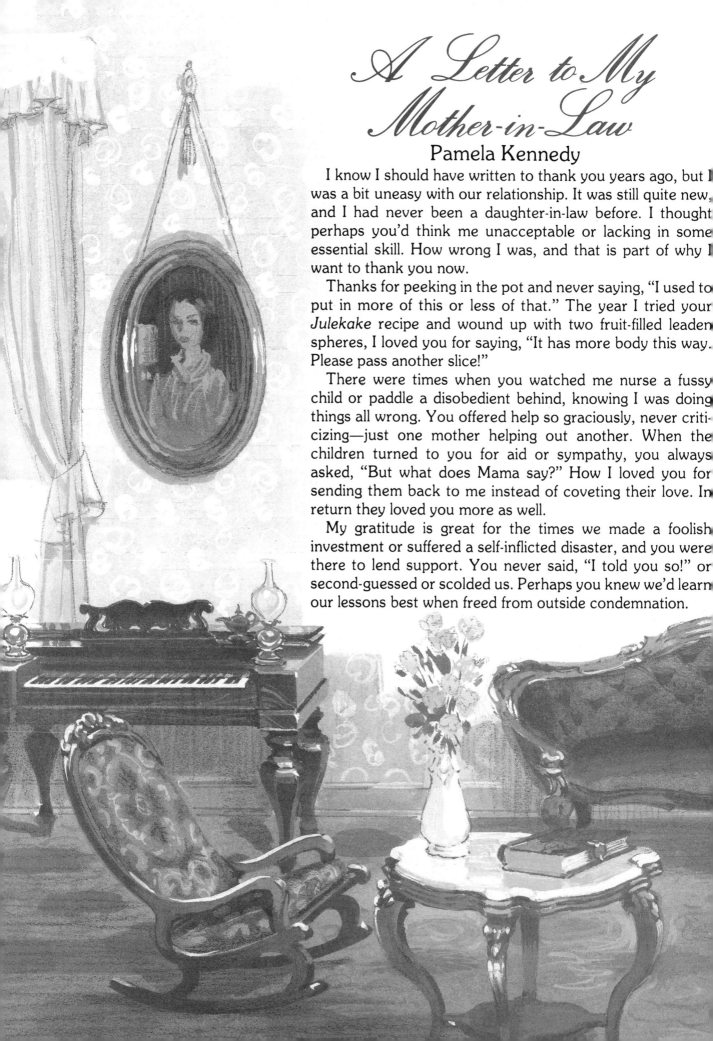

A Letter to My Mother-in-Law

Pamela Kennedy

I know I should have written to thank you years ago, but I was a bit uneasy with our relationship. It was still quite new, and I had never been a daughter-in-law before. I thought perhaps you'd think me unacceptable or lacking in some essential skill. How wrong I was, and that is part of why I want to thank you now.

Thanks for peeking in the pot and never saying, "I used to put in more of this or less of that." The year I tried your *Julekake* recipe and wound up with two fruit-filled leaden spheres, I loved you for saying, "It has more body this way. Please pass another slice!"

There were times when you watched me nurse a fussy child or paddle a disobedient behind, knowing I was doing things all wrong. You offered help so graciously, never criticizing—just one mother helping out another. When the children turned to you for aid or sympathy, you always asked, "But what does Mama say?" How I loved you for sending them back to me instead of coveting their love. In return they loved you more as well.

My gratitude is great for the times we made a foolish investment or suffered a self-inflicted disaster, and you were there to lend support. You never said, "I told you so!" or second-guessed or scolded us. Perhaps you knew we'd learn our lessons best when freed from outside condemnation.

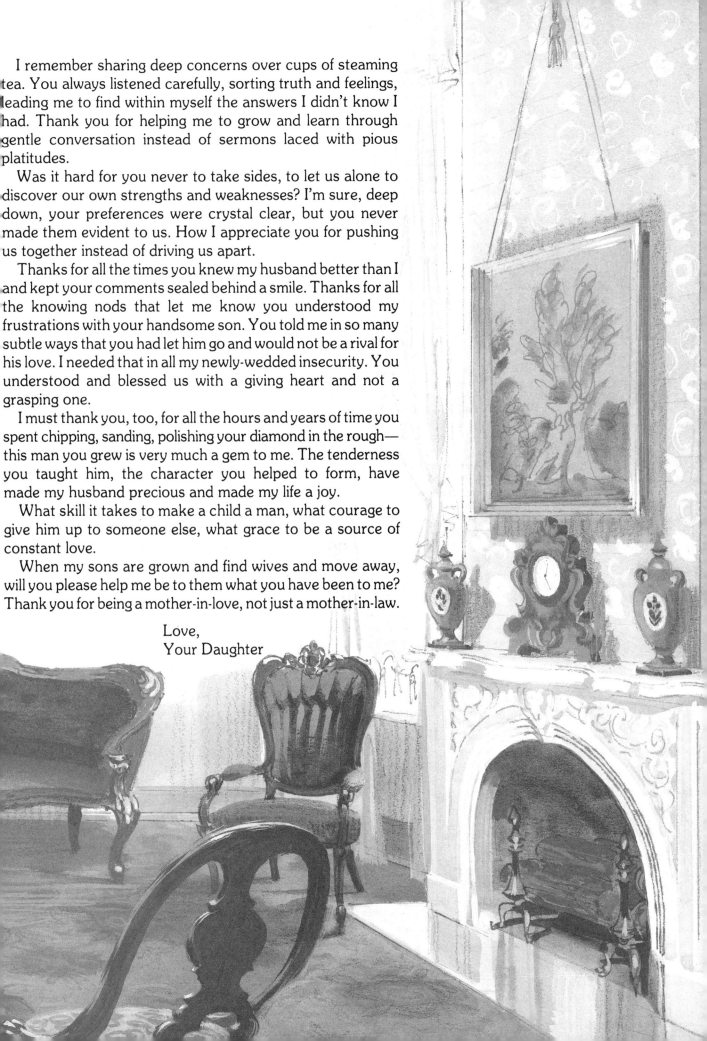

I remember sharing deep concerns over cups of steaming tea. You always listened carefully, sorting truth and feelings, leading me to find within myself the answers I didn't know I had. Thank you for helping me to grow and learn through gentle conversation instead of sermons laced with pious platitudes.

Was it hard for you never to take sides, to let us alone to discover our own strengths and weaknesses? I'm sure, deep down, your preferences were crystal clear, but you never made them evident to us. How I appreciate you for pushing us together instead of driving us apart.

Thanks for all the times you knew my husband better than I and kept your comments sealed behind a smile. Thanks for all the knowing nods that let me know you understood my frustrations with your handsome son. You told me in so many subtle ways that you had let him go and would not be a rival for his love. I needed that in all my newly-wedded insecurity. You understood and blessed us with a giving heart and not a grasping one.

I must thank you, too, for all the hours and years of time you spent chipping, sanding, polishing your diamond in the rough— this man you grew is very much a gem to me. The tenderness you taught him, the character you helped to form, have made my husband precious and made my life a joy.

What skill it takes to make a child a man, what courage to give him up to someone else, what grace to be a source of constant love.

When my sons are grown and find wives and move away, will you please help me be to them what you have been to me? Thank you for being a mother-in-love, not just a mother-in-law.

Love,
Your Daughter

Mother

I think God took the fragrance
Of a flower,
A flower, which blooms
Not for world praise,
But which makes sweet and
    beautiful some bower;
The compassion of the dew,
Which gently lays
Reviving freshness on the fainting earth
And gives to all the tired things
New birth;

The steadfastness and radiance of stars,
Which lift the soul above confining bars;
The gladness of fair dawns;
The sunset's peace;
Contentment, which from trivial rounds
Asks no release;
The life which finds its greatest joy
In deeds of love for others.
I think God took these precious things
And made of them mothers.

Author Unknown

A Rose for Mother

Another Mother's Day is here,
Bringing joy and pleasures new.
On this special day, Mother dear,
I want to remember you.

I cannot give you costly gifts,
And I've told you this before,
No matter what I give to you,
You give back much, much more.

I'm giving you a pure, sweet rose,
Gathered in the early morn;
This rose you planted in my heart
The day that I was born.

In kindly, loving thoughts of you,
And with the faith you still impart,
The rose I give to you today
Is the love that's in my heart.

Cleo M. Shoffstall

MOTHER'S ROSE
Bob Taylor

The Flower Lover

Her world is made of flowers,
Of blossoms the year round;
Her touch is as magic
To every spot of ground.

She knows the flower language
And speaks it fluently;
She understands flower souls,
Their rich eternal beauty.

Her springtime smiles through hyacinths,
Long-stemmed and flawless bright;
Her summer reveals roses,
That fragrance day and night.

And in her autumn garden
Banks a wealth of deep'ning shades,
Which the winter will transform
Into gorgeous white brocades!

Zelda Davis Howard

Mother's Garden

Mother is envied by the neighbors
For the flowers she has grown;
And they all say her garden
Is the loveliest they've known.
In early spring she will prepare
A fertile, sunny spot;
How carefully she marks the rows
And plants the seeds she bought.

It always seems to thrive and grow
Beneath her tender care,
For it is watered with her love
And nourished with a prayer.
God answers her with sun and rain,
And as the months go by,
The flowers bloom in radiant hues
Like rainbows in the sky.

Her prize bouquets are freely given
To those who chance to call,
But to the ill and lonely folks
She gives the best of all.
For brightening other people's lives
Is Mother's lifelong goal,
And the beauty of her flowers
Is reflected in her soul.

Reginald Holmes

When I Was a Child

I remember the stories
That dear Mother told
When I was a child
Of five years old.

They were tender and warm—
Little girl and boy tales—
Not the frightening type
With rattles and wails.

They were tales to remember
Through long growing years
That we could recall
And repeat to our dears.

They are old-fashioned now,
And outmoded, I know,
But still they bring back
A lingering glow.

If I had my wish,
It most surely would be
That my children remember
These same stories and me.

Edith M. Helstern

The Old Rocking Chair

While looking through the attic,
I spied it standing there,
And shining, happy memories
Sprang from that rocking chair.

I could see my mother rocking
By the lamplight every night
As I climbed into her lap
With a cozy, warm delight.

She would tell me lovely stories
And sing sweet lullabies;
With gentleness she'd hold me
Till I'd close my sleepy eyes.

Once again I saw her knitting
And how the needles flew
To make us pretty things
With yarn of vivid hue.

Then I seemed to see my mother
With folded hands in prayer,
As she did so many evenings
In her grand old rocking chair.

For just a little while,
All the magic past
Came back to bring me happiness
In a dream I wished would last.

That rocking chair is precious;
God blessed it from above.
It's the golden throne of Mother,
Where she shared her special love.

LaVerne P. Larson

Photo Overleaf
RURAL LIVING
Ken Dequaine

The Safety Net

"What do you think of when you hear the word 'mother'?"

This was asked recently by a friend who was trying to think of the perfect Mother's Day gift. I apologetically replied that I could not help. When I think of my mother, I don't think of roses or candy or cooking utensils. I think of courage and independence and understanding. These were the gifts she gave to me, and they are not easily represented by objects.

There was once a wild and stubborn six-year-old who loved the woods and would fly down animal paths in pursuit of imaginary friends or foes, never thinking once of snakes or traps or unskilled hunters. Mother let me go—but only so far. "Don't go past the firebreak. It's too dangerous." I thought Mother knew everything, so I listened. Most of the time. When I did pass beyond the firebreak, the excursions were hesitant and cautious. And brief.

There was the shy and timid ten-year-old who was extremely uncertain of her musical ability, but who desperately wanted to try out for the school band. "Try it," Mother urged. "You'll never know if you can unless you try." I faltered more than once, losing audition after audition, but I continued to try. By the time I was a senior in high school, I was an award-winning flute player.

"Try it for yourself. You'll never know if you don't try. Just remember, I'll always be here if you fail." This advice helped me through the roughest times of my life. It gave me the independence and courage I needed as a college freshman, as a new bride, as a new mother. As with most motherly advice, I had to grow up to understand and appreciate it. Only as an adult did I realize how hard it was for Mother to stand back and let me try things for myself. Only as an adult did I realize how difficult it was for her not to chase that six-year-old into

the woods. She was always there to comfort the pain of failure, but more importantly, she was brave enough to let the pain occur.

Mother was never able to keep me still long enough to teach me sewing or cooking. Instead, she gave me the independence and courage to learn them on my own. I might burn a few fingers, but she was always there with the salve. She taught me to fly while she held the net. The only way I can repay her is to fly high above the net and to pass on to my children the gifts of courage, understanding, and independence which she gave me. Flowers just aren't enough.

Thank you, Mother, for letting me go—and for teaching me how to fly.

Ramona Pope Richards

Her Garden

My mother had a garden
Where lovely flowers grew,
Sending out their fragrance
Drenched with morning dew.

Mother loved her garden;
She tended it with care,
Raking, hoeing, weeding
To keep it neat and fair.

She had another garden
That filled her life with joy;
It was the garden of her heart—
Each precious girl and boy.

This garden, planted with tender love,
Was no doubt sprinkled with tears,
But Mother reaped a sweet content
With the harvest of the years.

Violet Schoulda

Photo Oppo
GARDEN GATH
Monserrate Sc

A Mother Is Springtime

You are the music in the songs
That nature sings to earth;
You are the pattern of the stars,
The miracle of birth.

You are the wonder of the sky,
The enchantment of the sea.
You are the purity of air,
The calmness of the lea.

You are the magic of the night,
The glory of the day;
You are the mystery of time
That all of life conveys.

You are the freshness of the rain
That falls in early May,
The perfection of the rainbow
That shines in its array.

You are the beauty of the spring,
The hyacinth's perfume,
The fragrant honeysuckle;
You are the rose in bloom.

You are the summer's gentle breeze,
The bright sunrise at dawn,
The melody of singing birds,
The softness of the fawn.

You are the grandeur of the forest,
The stature of the trees,
The fairness of the lilies,
The honey from the bees.

You are richness of the hue
In autumn's golden glow;
You are the warmth in winter,
The whiteness of the snow.

You're all of life combined in one
In your charming, queenly ways.
Your life bespeaks the gift of love
To all who share your days.

Mary Pitchford Barnes

This Day Is Ours

This day is ours—this perfect day;
The sky is blue, the winds are gay.
    And every sunbeam seems to call:
    "Come out, come out! This day is all
The loveliness we know as May."

So short a while we have to play—
To race the winds that will not stay,
    But ere the gathering shadows fall,
        This day is ours.

Oh, let us take the rugged way
Where little trails run free and stray
    Through forests green and vast and tall,
    Where nature knows no fence or wall—
Out there where we can truly say
        This day is ours.

Mary E. Linton

In Fields of Green

In fields of green I watch the sky,
Where birds above me freely fly
On wings of peace, to realms unseen
By poorest lad, by richest queen.

In fields of green I watch the grass,
Where beneath my moving feet they pass,
Those flowers of God, whose fragrance goes
Where no one sees, where no one knows.

In fields of green I watch the day,
As ceaselessly it slips away.
This dawn shall ne'er again be seen;
This sunset ne'er again give sheen.

In fields of green this life goes by,
With first a smile, and then a sigh,
With a whispered prayer to a God who knows
The passions of life, its suns, its snows.

Margaret S. Wright

Have You Ever?

Have you ever gone out
    walking
On a lovely day in spring?
Have you ever paused to
    listen
To the song the wee brooks
    sing?

Have you ever searched for
    violets
In the woodlands where
    they grow,
Though it seems just
    yesterday
The ground was deep with
    snow?

Have you ever caught the
    gay notes
Of a robin way up high,

Or the soft whir from the
  wings
Of a hummingbird nearby?

Have you listened to a
  cricket
When the evening shadows
  fall?
For 'tis then you're sure to
  hear him
Near a fence or old stone
  wall.

Have you ever watched the
  twinkle
Of that first bright evening
  star?
Have you wondered why it
  winks at you
Above the world so far?

Have you ever stopped to
  ponder
At the beauty of it all?
And to say, "Dear God, I
  thank you;
You have made both great
  and small."

Jayne Burrier

The Promise Fulfilled

The meadow was whispering of spring today
As I walked her soft, green sod.
The song of the lark, as she built her nest,
Surrounded the pathway I trod.
A shimmering brook, loose of winter's bonds,
Danced over a pebble beach;
And cotton-puff clouds floated low in the sky,
Seemingly just out of reach.

The promise of birth, with all its joy,
Abounded on every side;
And the heart of the farmer
Was carefree and light
As he looked at his fields with pride.
Go into the meadow or climb the hill,
Seek out a restful place,
And watch the splendor of spring unfold
With all of its beauty and grace.

Shirley Sallay

Mayflowers

Halfway between the earth and sky
Spring's morn would find me climbing high,
Uncovering a treasure trove
From its sheltered, hidden grove.

Past fields held in by post and rail,
I'd follow a rocky winding trail.
And year by year my heart knew where
Mayflowers grew, sweet and fair.

Toylike scenes came into view;
A tiny train passed slowly through
A distant valley far below,
Past patchwork gardens in a row.

Wisps of smoke trailed through the trees
Sent by farms on the breeze.
In nearby lowland pastures stirred
A silent, moving grazing herd.

Then, searching in dry leaves of fall,
Beneath the spruce grove cool and tall,
I found pale pink mayflowers,
Fragrant, garlanding fir towers.

Halfway between the earth and sky
Spring's morn would find me climbing high.
How lovelier are things hardly won
Than those found easily in the sun.

Marilyn Alma Morin

A Mountain Tale

Once I found, deep in a wood,
Some jonquils springing up
(Where yesterday no blooms had stood),
Holding sunshine in each cup.

I asked a mountain man to tell
The story of this bed
Of secret flowers in a dell,
And this is what he said:

"They say that wise old Grandma Gray
Lives way up on that hill;
Alone she sees the creek at play
And hears the whippoorwill.

"She knows the possums and the crows;
She whispers to the bees.
And none can tell how much she knows,
How many things she sees.

"But when you find a glen that's filled
With sun-drenched daffodils,
That's where she tipped her churn and spilled
Her butter down the hills."

Margaret Jean Fuller

Silver Symphony

I hear a silver thread of song
Along the pasture fence,
Where saw-tooth briars the grasses lace
And hazel shrubs grow dense.
And there I spy the soft, gray breast
Of a field sparrow on her nest,

While higher up, among the leaves,
In measures short and long,
Needling a pattern in and out,
A feather-stitch of song,
Her mate pours out his silvery lay
To edge the bright green gown of May.

May Allread Baker

I Love Dandelions

"Psst. I love dandelions." This must be whispered quie[t] and quickly. I do not dare to proclaim this in public. I wou[ld] be ostracized by friends and neighbors.

My neighbors are usually gentle folk who tend their flow[er] beds, plant gardens, and socialize over the back fence, b[ut] every spring these same neighbors undergo a frighteni[ng] metamorphosis. They shed their gentle, unassuming exteric[rs] and become ruthless attackers. They advance armed wi[th] knives, shovels, picks, and poisons. They bribe small, defen[se] less children to help them; they use extreme methods [of] eradication. Neighbors who won't join the war are shunn[ed] and talked about in most uncomplimentary terms.

Who is this terrible foe? A small yellow flower. I cann[ot] understand why people spend days digging at dandelions spend days planting seeds that never sprout, plants th[at] don't produce, annuals that end, perennials that poop. Y[et] every spring—without fail—hundreds of these lovely da[n] delions appear without any preplanning, planting, or prunir[g.] These bright yellow buttons (the Chinese call them "yello[w] flowered-earth-nails") promise sunny, summer days ahead[.]

I'm not the only one who likes dandelions. Pioneer wome[n,] homesick for their eastern homes, planted tiny plots [of] dandelions on the rolling prairies of the West. Gophe[rs,] prairie dogs, pheasants, goldfinches, and sparrows eat da[n] elion seeds. Rabbits, chipmunks, deer, and porcupines eat the plants. Indians and early settlers ate the greens as vegetables and used them to make medicines. They roasted the roots to make a coffee-like beverage.

Dandelions are definitely good to eat, and who am I to criticize free food? Young leaves, cut before the bud develops, can be used in salads or as greens. Farmers around Vineland, New Jersey, even grow them as a cash crop. Have you tried dandelion wine?

Children love to blow the fluffy seed heads (they don't realize the germination rate is often ninety percent, even if the neighbors do). Kids make yards and yards of dandelion chains from the hollow stems, and how can you tell if a friend likes butter if you don't hold a dandelion under his chin? And what mother's heart doesn't melt when a toddler sticks out a chubby handful of dandelions and says "I love you."

You can even send a message to your beloved by whispering into the dandelion puffball. When you blow all the seeds away at once, the message will be carried to your loved one. If only one seed remains, that means your lover is thinking of you.

Dandelions are not as useless as my neighbors seem to think. I just smugly smile and go about my business as they carry on their war, for I know (and so do they—deep in their hearts) that they can't win. Dandelion tap roots can extend more than three feet into the earth, bringing up enriching minerals to help the soil. New plants start if any root is left.

"Wage war," I say, "but the dandelion will live forever, and it is about time for them to stand up and be counted!"

Carol Hammond

Celebrate America with *ideals*

From north to south, east to west, the grandeur and variety of America are exciting and fascinating. In our next issue, *Countryside,* we explore the best and brightest parts of the North American continent. Join us and browse through brilliant full-color photographs of our shining coasts, lush river valleys, and snowy mountain peaks. We also will take a close look at the people and ideas which add luster to our *Countryside.* Share in the celebration, and perhaps you will agree with Mrs. Hortense B. Michelsen of Murphy, North Carolina, who writes, "Your magazine is inspirational, uplifting, beautifully illustrated, and an honor to receive," or Ms. D. Jean A. Martin of Cheektowaga, New York, who writes:

> I have just recently received my first publication of *Ideals.* I surely never expected to receive such an interesting, informative magazine. Plus the illustrations and photos are just beautiful. Now, once I have read every page from cover to cover, I will look forward to the next issue with much anticipation. *Ideals* has a permanent resting place in our living room for all to see.

Thank you, Mrs. Michelsen and Ms. Martin! You, too, can share our celebration by giving a subscription to a friend, starting with our next issue, *Countryside.*

ACKNOWLEDGMENTS

SILVER SYMPHONY was reprinted from *THE GIFT OF THE YEAR* by May Allread Baker, copyright 1964, The Brethren Press, Elgin, Illinois. Used by permission. THIS DAY IS OURS by Mary E. Linton, from her book *ON WINGS OF THE SOUL,* copyright 1947 by Burton Publishing Company; copyright © 1960 by Mary E. Linton. Used by permission of the author. I PLANTED MY GARDEN TODAY by Mamie Ozburn Odum, from her book *BITS OF SOUTHERN SUNSHINE.* Used by permission of the author. MOTHER MONTH by Margaret Rorke, from *CHRISTMAS COULD—BE TALES (AND OTHER VERSES),* copyright © 1984 by Northwood Institute Press. Used by permission. Our sincere thanks to the following whose addresses we were unable to locate: Jayne Burrier for HAVE YOU EVER?; Margaret Jean Fuller for A MOUNTAIN TALE; the estate of Reginald Holmes for MOTHER'S GARDEN; the estate of Zelda Davis Howard for THE FLOWER LOVER; Mildred Moon Howell for THE MEANING OF MOTHER; Brenda Leigh for I WISH I'D KNOWN MY MOTHER WHEN...; Marilyn Alma Morin for MAYFLOWERS; Mary Lynn Nelson for SIXTEEN; Violet Schoulda for MOTHER'S GARDEN; Cleo M. Shoffstall for A ROSE FOR MOTHER; Mary Quimby Sine for A MOTHER'S DREAMS...; Helen Louise Williams for MY GARDEN from her book *OF ALL THINGS,* copyright 1955; Kay Wissinger for MOTHER'S KITCHEN; Margaret S. Wright for IN FIELDS OF GREEN.